The Little Donkey with Hidden Destiny

by
Jacqueline Bailey

Copyright© 2022

by Jacqueline Bailey

All rights reserved.

Cover & Book Designed by

TRUTH Communications Media & Publications

TruthCommunications.org

The contents of this book may not be reproduced, duplicated or transmitted without direct written permission from the autor or the publisher. Under no circumstances will any blame or legal responsibility be held against the publisher, or author, for any damages, reparation, or monetry loss neither directly not indirectly due to information contained within this book.

Published by TRUTH Communications Media & Publications

Printed in Canada

ISBN 978-1-7776796-5-1

Dedication

To my children, my grandchildren

and great grandchildren.

I pray you enjoy many years of fun reading.

There was a little donkey named Tsair who lived in Jerusalem. Tsair was the youngest and smallest of a family of five. Tsair's family had the important job of carrying food to the King's palace.

But because Tsair was the smallest of his family, there wasn't much he could help with. He was tied to a post and left there most days, while his mum, dad and brothers went off to work.

Tsair had two good friends who were flies named Met and Nik. As he stood in his usual place one hot afternoon, his friends flew over and sat on his ear.

"Shalom," said Met and Nik together. "What exciting thing have you done today?" And they both laughed.

"Oh, go away," said the little donkey crossly. "I'm not in the mood for your jokes."

"Oh my, whatever is wrong with you, Tsair? We were only joking," said Met.

Tsair hung his head and said, "I'm sorry, guys. I didn't mean to yell at you."

"I can see you are having a bad day," said Met.
"Would you like to tell us what is bothering you?"

Tsair sighed deeply and said, "Yes, it has been a bad day.
and I think my owner wants to get rid of me."

Met and Nik said quickly, "Oh no, you're mistaken. You are a part of a family, and I'm sure he won't separate you from the others."

My owner doesn't want me, "said Tsair. "He told our neighbor I am a waste of hay and water."

"I am sorry to hear that, my friend, "replied Nik.
"Why would he say such a thing?" asked Met.

"I guess he's tired of feeding me,
and I'm not being useful," said Tsair.

"We can understand how you feel," said Met
"Most people see us flies as a bother. We are called useless and annoying. Oh yes, we know how much those words can hurt. But do remember our Creator has a reason for every creature he created, and we have heard the stories of how our ancestors helped bring a great and arrogant king to his knees. The King had made the people of Israel, which God loves very much, his slaves. So God sent a huge army of us flies as a plague on his land to make the king set the Israelites free."

Isair shook his head, laughed, and said, "Thank you for trying to make me feel better."

Met and Nik replied, "What are friends for?"
They both joined in his laughter.

Nik said, "Since you are feeling better, we will be off now!"

"Where are you off to?" asked Tsair.

"We are going to the temple," said Nik. "There are so many people in Jerusalem these days, and the temple is packed with man and beast."

"Ok, but be careful," said Tsair. "Many people means many hands trying to swat you!"

"We will be careful. Goodbye!" Nik and Met said as they flew off.

Tsair watched as they flew out of sight,
then lowered his head to take a drink of water.

As he drank from the trough, lost in
his thoughts, he was startled when his mum
let out a very loud bray.
He turned, spilling the water
as he looked at her.

"What's wrong?" he asked.

"There are two men across the street talking to each other and watching us," she said. "I think they want to steal us."

Tsair craned his neck around her as he looked for the men. As he stared at them, they began to walk in his direction. Tsair felt a bit of fear in his tummy, and he drew closer to his mum.

She was unsettled too, and she walked back and forth as far as her rope allowed.

Tsair started to bray as loudly as he could to scare the men away.

But the men reached them soon enough and came around to Tsair's side to untie his rope. As Tsair struggled to pull away, his owner came outside.

On seeing the men with his donkeys, he asked, "What are you doing untying my donkey?"

The men replied, "The master needs him."

To Tsair's surprise, his owner stepped back and allowed the men to untie his rope.

Tsair was very frightened, and he struggled to get free.

Tsair asked his mum, "Do you know this master that these men speak of?"

She replied, "It's a man called Jesus. He has the whole of Jerusalem in an uproar."

"How has he done that?" asked Tsair.

"Well, he keeps saying God, our Creator, is his father. He also called the religious leaders of the people, the Pharisees and Sadducees hypocrites, because they didn't do the good works that they told the people they must do to be holy."

"What?" exclaimed Tsair. "He said that to their faces?"

"Yes, he did," said his mum, "and that's not all. He has healed the sick, blind, deaf, and lame, even on the Sabbath. He is kind to everyone, but the religious leaders don't like him and are always looking to pick fights with him. He also allowed a woman who lived a sinful life to wash his feet while he was dining, which caused quite a talk."

"Why?" asked Tsair.

"Well, some consider him a religious leader, so allowing such a sinful person to touch him is not right in the eyes of the Pharisees and Sadducees."

"Was she a bad person?" asked Tsair.

"No," she replied. "What she did was bad, but the master told her she was forgiven, which made her very happy. She was so happy, she wanted to wash Jesus' feet, which were tired and dusty from his long walk."

Tsair began to think he did not have to fear the man called Jesus, so he stopped pulling on the rope and even quickened his pace.

The man turned to look at him and smiled. He said, "Good boy, little one, let's hurry to the master."

The little donkey began to think about his meeting with Jesus. I'm small and not very strong. How will I be of use to such a man? Tsair was so caught up in his thoughts he didn't realize they had reached the place where Jesus stood.

As he looked around at the men in the crowd, he knew which one was the master. He felt the love and kindness coming from him.

Jesus reached out and rubbed Tsair's head gently and said, "Thank you for your service this day, my strong friend." Someone threw a cloth on his back, and Jesus climbed on and gently nudged Tsair to start walking.

As he walked along the street, people threw palm branches
and clothes on the road for him to walk on.
Although he had never had anyone sit on his back
or be in such a large crowd, Tsair felt peaceful.

The clothes and branches were hitting
him in his face at times, and people
were jumping around and shouting,
but the little donkey was not afraid.
He felt strong and believed
he could take Jesus to
the place he was
going safely.

Tsair soon realized they were going to the temple. When they reached the steps, Jesus stopped and climbed down.

He patted Tsair on his side and smiled at him, then turned to walk up the temple steps.

For the first time in his life, Tsair felt important. As the man who brought him to Jesus took the rope and started to walk him back to his home, the young donkey looked at the ground because he couldn't feel the earth under him and thought he was floating.

When Tsair looked up, they were close to his home. His owner was standing by the shed waiting for them.

The man gave the rope to his owner and said, "Thank you for the use of your animal. He was a very brave donkey."

He then turned and walked back in the direction of the temple.

Tsair's owner looked at the little donkey. With a big smile on his face, he said, "You did well, little guy. You will be remembered for this." He patted Tsair on his head, tied the rope to the post and went inside the house.

A while later, he returned with some apples and gave them to Tsair. "You deserve a special treat for your bravery today," he said.

The donkey softly butted his owner on the leg and turned to eat the apples. As he was chewing, his friends, Met and Nik, flew over to him, buzzing with excitement.

"Tsair, Tsair!" they called to him at the same time.

Tsair swallowed the food in his mouth and replied, "Yes, what is it? What is all the excitement about?"

"Oh, you would not believe what we saw today, my friend. It was amazing and crazy all at the same time!"

"What happened?" asked Tsair.

"Have you heard of the man called Jesus?" asked Met. "I'm sure you have. All of Jerusalem is talking about him."

"I have heard of him," Tsair replied.

"Well, he came into Jerusalem today. The people went crazy. They were screaming his name and shouting Hosana, throwing their clothes and palm branches on the ground for the donkey carrying him to walk on," Nik explained. "Then he went into the temple and threw the money changers' tables over.

He chased the people that were buying and selling out of the temple with a whip because they were making the temple a marketplace. He was so angry, shouting at the priest and commanding them to stop making his father's house a den of thieves instead of a house of prayer.

It was really something to see."

The two flies stopped buzzing around and landed on Tsair's post, waiting for his reaction to the news.

With a shake of his head, the little donkey said, "I knew Jesus was there because I took him."

Met and Nik stared at each other, then looked at Tsair and said, "What did you just say?"

"I'm the one who took him to the temple," Tsair replied.

"How did you do that?" asked Met.
"What happened?" asked Nik.

Tsair told them about the men taking him from his post, meeting Jesus, and how he rode on Tsair's back to the temple.

Met and Nik were silent.

Tsair asked, "Do you think I'm lying?"
The flies immediately said, "No. We believe you! We're just shocked our little friend was chosen for this journey."

"I'm still shocked myself," Tsair replied. "I can't believe I was chosen for such a task, but now I know I am important and that my Creator has a purpose for me. Yes, I am small and not very strong, but I was available, and that is what Jesus needed me to be."

Met and Nik looked at their friend with awe. "We're so glad you see how special you are," they said. "We always knew it, and now you do too. We have to go now, but we will be back tomorrow to hear this story again."

"And I will enjoy telling it as many times as you like," said Tsair.

The flies said their goodbyes and flew off. Tsair went back to chewing his apples as he thought about the day he had. It started badly, but what a finish!

With a smile on his face, the little donkey lay down to take a nap.

www.ingramcontent.com/pod-product-compliance
Lightning Source LLC
Chambersburg PA
CBHW042107090526
44590CB00004B/130